Nistanimera

Peter Hughes was born in Oxford in 1956, and now lives on the Norfolk coast with his wife Lynn, in a coastguard cottage which is creeping ever closer to the cliff edge. Music, painting and writing have all been important to him over the years and he has tried to keep active in all of them, while still earning a living by teaching. In 2007 he left teaching to concentrate on his writing and several projects are currently unfolding in small-press publications and webzines. The cover of this book features one of his paintings.

Also by Peter Hughes

The Interior Designer's Late Morning, Many Press 1983
Bar Magenta (with Simon Marsh), Many Press, 1986
Odes on St. Cecilia's Day, Poetical Histories, 1990
The Metro Poems, Many Press, 1992
Psyche in the Gargano, Equipage, 1995
Paul Klee's Diary, Equipage, 1995
Keith Tippet Plays Tonight, Maquette Press, 1999
Blueroads: Selected Poems, Salt Publishing, 2003
Sound Signals Advising of Presence, infernal methods, 2006
Minor Yours, Oystercatcher Press, 2006

Peter Hughes

Nistanimera

Shearsman Books
Exeter

First published in in the United Kingdom in 2007 by
Shearsman Books Ltd
58 Velwell Road
Exeter EX4 4LD

www.shearsman.com

ISBN 978-1-905700-28-8

Acknowledgements
Some of these poems appeared in *Active in Airtime, Fire, The Gig, Great Works, Shadow Train, Tears in the Fence, 10th Muse* and *Tremblestone*. 'Oystercatcher', along with some other marine excursions, appeared in the chapbook *Sound Signals Advising of Presence* from infernal methods. 'Minor Yours' appeared as a chapbook from Oystercatcher Press.

The publisher gratefully acknowledges financial assistance for its 2005-2007 publishing programme from Arts Council England.

Contents

for Lynn

Six Klee Paintings

1920 Moonlit Night

the new formalism is always the former prison
the deepening rut worn out
by relentless pacing to & fro
another channel for the water
which already has every tune in its head
      you know where you are with a hoover
      you can locate your marbles
& be firm with one Dr Scholl
dovetailed to the starting block
      although blue is still blue
      as in a 1920 moonlit night
the sealed beam can't exhale
who's treading the perimeter
the grey juice of walking vision
eyelid thickness
all else out of sight
      & mindless
fins cross
an inner sheen
of dark grass

1923 Child in a Landscape

whatever dug this valley
has probably finished its lunch
no need for some new tidal myth
the sea goes in & out don't we all
meanwhile the stream is playing
conkers with its rocks
& applauding voluminously
you & the landscape stand inside each (other
& our musty ragged separation stands
what it can & cans what it must

yes look at the moon) too

1924 Portrait of Madame P

I like to think of gravitons
they are better than tooth-fairies
you carted my rootball no distance at all
though you looked like a wheelbarrow
on its last legs
the window sticks still
the point is already everywhere
& the line is the discharge of tension
between a couple of points
then before you know it it's lunch again
& four points make a fork
people you never knew
admire the upside-down boat on your head
physicists prefer to talk of prongs

1926 The Menagerie Goes on Parade

I dreamt I made a go-cart with Hart Crane
we called it Blue – my was it faithful
it carried Joni Mitchell
Miles Davis the Reverend Blue Hummock
Hilda Baker polishing a big plank of fluorspar
(we passed chandeliers malnutrition & a brass band
at the back of the lead-mine – the underground
years pressfluffed in your shirt pocket)
Blue Mitchell on trumpet with Horace Silver
thumping the dunnock
bobbing along on a staccato patter
of cats' eyes over the crest of the hill
into the final Prussian blue miles
& this darkening blue into which you drive
is the night inside you can't overtake

1928 A Page from the City's Records

the dark & steadfast star
stamped on your forehead
rustles town with windy
black-hole rumours
the sewage outlet religious
icon political badge
the full-stop at the end
of missing sentences
the blackball
ten billion dollars a week
a lot of arms
a lot of empty mouths
the O in the core
of all aesthetics
before you speak the day's out

1936

black
the queen of colours

only just before the end
did the distances
compress our chests
& flower within us as nettles

we were peopled
by great silences

hard to resist the inside of your wrist
even in this little crowd of human beings
backdrops cardboard rocks & red wine

delicate flicks big wet licks spilt stickiness
emulsion under the nails & between finger-tips
we knocked up Oz in a couple of hours

after months of battening down hatches
keeping shutters closed
checking locks

the whole caboodle gets blown away
then slides down a rainbow
into this space between streets

next thing I know
you're smiling down from the top turret
unfurling your flag over the emerald city

I wiped some of your green off my arm
but all your other colours
have seeped in deep & gone bronze

Oystercatcher

I

a load of gutted loft insulation
stirs on the front lawn

an airy cake of yellow web & dust

we & the strange house
breathe in slight differences
through late winter nights
that resound to little adaptations
& imagined trespasses

the space above has increased

the January morning is a shallow basket
left by the dustbin
weightless
full of snow & brilliant tracks

2

the chalk stratum glows
between thunder & carrstone

a low tide behind
the sea wind come to life

3

a chimney unblocked
after 20 years

voices return
from undressed walls

it dawns on us
the oceanic surge through
seconds of disrupted grammar
the sea wielding sun
to open windows

4

shifting whispers of sky in the hearth
taste of stale air in cupboards

relative absence of paranoia

5

sticks of rot & woodworm
feed the reopened hearth

ease this decayed air out of the house &
mouth into the local star gale

6

the winds walking
waves on the sea

through the carpet
right to the fire

on the horizon
a white citadel

7

February quarter light & dawn smell
Rustin's Pure Turpentine
150 mil of titanium white
the last smear of indigo
breadcrumbs & linseed oil

the ache of the familiar versus
the ache of the unknown

the day's first oystercatcher lands
facing east

8

mussel beds sunk under the storm
top of the world whipped headless black

noise as of boxes being shifted
way below or above

hair-dark wind

9

trudging back off the low-tide mussel beds
a muddy Tesco bag full of late sun
& two pints of living shells

the making tide & blue angels
go about their business as usual

you can walk here so far into the sea
that when you turn around
the land appears
like someone else's and your own idea

the tide is going out
two in the morning

between you
& the moon

rocks seething
beach coated in a glow

I'm hanging on
by the skin
of your
teeth

October 22

(for James K. Baxter)

You made your way down the valley
finding yourself on unfamiliar tracks,

a cemetery path that kinked away
from October, between a cosily

vicious bonfire gnawing sticks of bluegum,
& the stone angel in the corner.

I see you still heading for that window light,
Pyrrha pounding in your pulse & lines.

I still see you drinking deeply, leaning back,
smashing your glass on the world.

United Nations

your tongue shone like green leather –
your jade crucifix earring burned
under the street lamp

soon it will be spring
but not before many more deaths
ruched in fields of ice and hunger

dropped by night in this dawn nothing
& you white insoluble equations
I walk for hours

veering back at each outskirt
of the city beside myself
the sound of many footsteps

of all the people, histories & things
I could put in my mouth
the hungriest is this pale light

Liederkreis

I

morning appears like a
disappointing Heine website
moving towards the window
away from leaden pillows
she walks beyond horizons
of echoey b-sides

after dark we stand on
exposed & disused inner runways
the cold night marries
arctic depths inside our chests

2

I duck in & out of rain
searching for a gap in time
it won't be long now
is where I live
I pay the rising costs with philosophy
today I pulled the chain
on one of the holy wells of the self
I let a key slip into the drain
through the shining water running in the gutter
I made for the heartening glow below street level
escaping from the fog of Prague
into the arbitrary place for food & drink
I have become

3

no sooner do I feel the urge to leave
via the wonderfully decaying woods
than you confront me in my mouth
& stars bristle in my veins

how does the blackthorn make those lines

I keep breathing in
measuring the bleak expanding heavens

these trees would hold my grief
on the damp tips of their dark branches
but I jealously swallow it down
packing it tight inside my bones

4

finger my heart again
can you feel the footsteps echo in its cell
that bastard builder death lives there
bodging up a post-retirement nook

the endless racket has kept me awake
for longer than I remember
I wish the idle sod would get on with it
let me turn into sleep once & for all

5

you picturesque crib of misery
you mausoleum of my ease
my great town it's time for me
to say the toughest of goodbyes

goodbye to each burnished junction
where still she passes by
goodbye to that shining site
where I first saw her

I wish I'd never met you,
beautiful queen of my heart
then it wouldn't have ended this way
with me so inside out & out to dry

I never hoped to touch your heart
I never even wished for love
I just wanted to live a quiet life
inside the same air that you breathe

but you drive me away
your lips mouth cruel words
madness swarms through my body
its eggs hatching out in the wrecked hutch of my heart

I plod on with my heavy sack of self
& this worn out staff
until I put my head down in the distance
the cold hole fitting perfectly for ever

Workshop

Sometimes you just take a big white clod
shake it off, hold it up to the air
rotating it deftly, or otherwise.
Sometimes you have to scrape features out
with split clogged nails.
Violent hurling to the ground has been known
to release patterns of impact,
spread & tail recalling galaxies.
Hours of pounding can render it
amenable to blending with squirts
of foreign matter, cheesy pastes.
Then you get the momentary vacancies
when you breathe all over it, not
noticing its diminution till it's melted
evaporated & condensed on the windows
obstructing the light, hiding the view.
Once in a blue moon you come back in
from the kitchen & it's written itself.

Starfish

ochre orange mauve
a small implied vortex
its chubby roughness
sags damp on the wet sand
at the mid-tide
apparently lifeless
in the westering sun

yet when lifted into the light
each tube foot started
walking through the dusk air
towards the future

Dichterliebe

I

in the bloodcurdling month of May
when cells & hearts were bursting
my cardboard box was turned
entirely inside out

in the unearthly month of May
when birds stumble under hedgerow plants
my heart unfurled
like a hedgehog in a pile of dry leaves
which she approached with Swan Vestas

2

I swallowed the spring
& the spring swallowed me

my breath became caves in the sky
caverns and cathedrals
sculpted from the songs of blackbirds

3

burgundy sauvignon the fringe the light
once I loved them all in freefall
now I don't I just love
that neat superb unpolluted whole woman
she's the out-of-body experience in a body
the deep red the dry white
the soft fringe the bright light
the letting it breathe the swallowing deep

4

when I look into you looking
my body eases itself into my body
then when I get to kiss your mouth
I am all a fertile vowel farm

when I let myself down slightly
onto your breasts I celebrate like
a new Chelsea signing but when
the talk turns to love my head is eased
into this office shredder

5

I would dunk my soul
into a glass of chablis
the wine would lisp some old changes
worked round 'Body & Soul'

the warm saliva solo would vibrate
like the kiss from her mouth
in that silent & unforgettable gig
we shared when time was of the essence

Peg

under the massive and still frost free
scintillation of piercing stars

the dog sits in a mild October gale
under the energised band of the milky way

demented with night

unwilling to come back
into the caravan

The Dying Bishop Anticipates Heaven

I've never been much of a one
for harps & choral music –
sitting in tight-arsed rows
waiting for a break in the strumming
    to go & gnaw wholefoods.

Nor do I fancy
hovering & simpering
        simultaneously.

I see heaven as more of a
languid blow-job enjoyed
while eating Weetabix
soaked in half a bottle of Bailey's
to Dusty Springfield's Greatest Hits.

    Or was that Weymouth?

Off the Map

Tuscan gulley of wheat and olives
  breathless in the brazen pause of summer
the track curving down & away
  two dusty white lines
hot tread of greying tyres

  either side of bushy reservation
grasses & leaves bent whispering
  against the sump of the crawling car
small kisses down the abdomen
  weeds shifting on distant plots

Landing

First July light covered our sea with birds.
More than ever before rode the morning,
moving with a rhythm from the distance –
the bay, the chalk & sandstone, the moon's ghost.

Where do you stop? You stand on the landing
glowing between the front & back windows,
breathing in quiet light & making tide.
Life finally fits, like wine in a glass.

& before the birds rise, & tide withdraws,
you realize the tide is always high,
the great wish of sea, reaching for the moon,
staying constant as the Earth turns through it.

John Forbes in Efes

Your bent Loughborough handlebars rusted
while you sat with Rod Mengham in one hand,
an unusual kebab in the other.
Distinctive features dissolved in the red,
memory as close to the bone as this
cold textured indigo of moonlit ground.
I don't know how the conversation turned
to DIY and timber composites:
chipboard, MDF and the 4-ply which,
you observed, might well precede coition.
Craftspersonship, an arterial wit,
fathomless commitment to bloody art –
you pay the bill with immense courtesy
you grumpy old sod: 'the night's still young'.

Minor Yours

I

I'm a charcoal sketch
a self portrait in an unframed mirror
a subterranean rumour
a trickle of coal dust
down an outhouse wall
a dog digging in the sand
then scratching its ear till it bleeds

political refugee & asylum seeker
my refuge is my trumpet & you
ancient city of Lynn

I sit in the low cavern
of your expectations
inhaling slowly
so as not to choke on the sooty air
that's filled my head for weeks

it's better not to unpack

just a bottle & a book

the horn & the music
keep the corners of your lips firm
& the centre relaxed

the grittiness of the familiar
dissolving in dank unfamiliar acres

diaphragm & embouchure:
ha hu he

certain African hunters would bury
a belonging in a secret place
far from home
so if home vanished
soul would not

2

outside
the community of our perceptions
the mind's amblings   tracks full of moisture
bone & glowing edges
the mind never clearing except
to arrange its core as a clearing
a woven nest of scraps & texts
notes & grasses   Kenny Dorham
breaking my heart like the glimpsed deer
of my next wordless lyric fleeing
a pattering sound underfoot
or in the background
sometimes causes
sometimes registers anxiety
other times it gives the beat
you need to get up & move at all
pa te pa te pa te te pa te
with the tangle of purpose cut off behind you
& the massive magnet of habit
ditched in a skip off Station Road

we stand on the borders of earshot

the trumpet is the voice of the heart
stand up straight but tilt the instrument downwards
it is OK if some phrases sound like moon river
stop wriggling & shrugging   a dreaming dog
twisting your mouth at the mouth piece:
raise the trumpet & play what you feel
what you desire   what you feel & desire

are precisely what is required for redemption
the politics of our collective need for water & touch
lower the trumpet then do it again
the couple that moved out of here
kept arguing & she was crying over
leaving a small pet in the flower bed

3

purposeful steps
usually kill an insect or two
you can hear them in the attic
or in the alley down the side of the house
maybe it's a neighbour's dog   a fox
or some less easily named
nocturnal presence

you can hold any note like an inner vapour trail
or cantilevered out over the darkness
perhaps that last step when walking the plank
or a sudden acceleration extending the line of the Metro
by an act of breath alone far past the final station

then your right boot descends from space to clay
on the other side of one of a hundred misconceptions

even foreign earth sticks to the feet as you
walk to a familiar rhythm & put on weight
gravity loves you forever
sometimes you can shut up & listen

da du dee da du dee soft tongue legato dee du da

I've buried a spare & battered
mouthpiece taped up in a plastic bag
in a field on the outskirts of town

4

the road under the wheels   shadows
from an avenue of trees count the seconds
300 books' worth of petrol
to move an empty bookcase & a mongrel
from one side of town to the other

sell the car 10 minutes from the coast
leave half the contents outside the Sense shop

drink all night then catch the early bus
lit up against the wet dark dawn like a hallucination
to the station

the train shows no sign of stopping
at the edge of the continent

walk old dogs & weed for the housebound
pull pints in the Anchor or Crufts Nitespot
the Con Club & Matalan
clean their sacred spaces
from 6 a.m. till the shops open
double tongue ti ki ti ki ti ki ti ki
dogs can hear you all the way to Boston

5

time to clean out the pipes &
listen to the dripping in the cellar

then wait around for a computer
in the library on afternoons off
where the heating purrs
without consuming funds for food & Lidl wine

in there they write for you
with candour & respect for thought
they write with warmth
& they write in our languages

whilst back in the empty address
we hear the dripping
in the pipes of our heads
& bite back tremors
as the inexplicable sweat
trickles down our backs

in the horn of Africa big animals are almost
lifted away on evening breezes
they are so light with drought

here the TV sweats damp
behind the pictures of sand
& the dog stares at the ceiling

I dreamt a nest woven from soft
bright pulses of light & acknowledgement

in the heart of the internet
distant from all streets
& speaking to me in words we might recognise

6

open the back door into the dark garden
& stand in the concrete yard with the dog
follow the alley round to the front path
where the bin goes

there is no one key to all this
the front door back door the split bin & stars
a garage full of someone else's stuff
& what you finger as you go back in:
an unfamiliar key with no purpose
that you keep warm between your fingers

I have never stopped composing
tapping my toes invisibly inside my shoes
even during questioning in the 1950s cell
or touching two fingers together
as the wind lives or dies

half-pissed on leftovers
the TVs in a shopwindow remind me
of lyrics foreign to this city
sung by friends   relatives
or shabby celebrities across the world
ha hu he   da du dee   ti ki ti ki   da
my clothes smell of the smoke
& perfumes of others –
next summer I want to dry them in the sun
thank God for those strangers
who smile at us in the old way
& the half-familiar German supermarkets
standing ankle deep in British city

7

pros & cons   light & dark
your turn   my turn
unusually packaged antibiotics
a stunning range of pet foods to suit all tastes
we painted behind the sink
with half a tin of Duracoat
left over at work as Chet Baker
played *Minor Yours* with Art Pepper

we pick gristle from grey salami
& share hard olives
stuffed with some underwater flesh
I couldn't recognise

my brother locked in a
reception centre off the A14

we make love to the music
of the neighbours' radio
& the Chinese farmworkers' talk
as they get out of the Transit
& smoke for a while
in a wind off the North Sea
double tongue fast di gi di gi di gi
an entire nervous system in G minor
hanging out on this line

8

vicious & sympathetic by turns
the rhythms of the street   the square
the riverside path when the last bars close
we get the curtains drawn
open some Aldi vodka & chocolate
nicer than perpetual English wartime versions
& a tin of Troy with added rabbit

we turn on the wet telly
& watch people sell things from skips
for the price of brandy

you don't see the bombings
or the aftermath or any explanation

we skewer pale artichoke hearts
in the tin & watch the electric fire

we used to cook fresh artichokes
in the ashes of olive prunings
through long summer evenings

I remember it & so do you
da du dee pa te te pa
& neither of us will mention it
for some time   or perhaps ever

9

catch a hint of Cole Porter which isn't
& get out of the house into luxurious
rhythms of walking in the world
like a person living in the place where they live
where no-one is watching or measuring
setting you up to shoot at the target of yourself
reviewing evaluating chewing statistics
for lunch: out of the house along
the terraced street up past the
monumental church built on millenia
of rinsed river gravels & domestic refuse
trodden down as restless foundations
for the costly blocks of St Margaret's
slip through the ship-owners' narrow lanes
to the side of the river then north   upstream
to the few yellowing bones & scales –
what's left of the fishing fleet
peeling & rusting against the west bank
the tide low & the sky high
the dog is my only philosopher
wagging its body & keeping its tail still
Tomasz Stanko plays in my head till dawn

10

a sound heard when waking or sleeping
could be a door closing   someone entering
or leaving   some kind of signal
the dog grumbling to be let out

the hallway full of junkmail & piss
from the BNP

I listen to The Soul of Things
then Suspended Night

there is no hurry now
only a terrible urgency

I sold the trumpet months ago
after three guys stopped me in the street

one said
what are you wearing that fucking coat for?

I replied carefully *I'm cold*
& they broke my mouth & ribs anyway
with bare hands & fashionable footwear

this big neurotic moon
rushes alongside clouds
& non-existent trains

the sea is loud tonight
the tide high & light-headed
on Easter moonshine
the currents go around
the bend littered with
party food for monsters

dogs are standing up
in unlit kitchens
gloomy hallways
& shifting gardens
all over the world
with a gleam in each eye

I play Clifford Brown &
Miles until they die

it is one of those nights
that's come off its spindle
quietly eased off its hinges
but no-one has yet noticed

though the dogs are waiting
with reflections in their eyes
for someone to tell them

this is not happening
& someone will come back

The Radio Sonnets

This sequence of poems consists of words taken from the *Radio Times* for the week beginning Saturday 8th April 2006.

The order in which the words are used is the same as the order in which they originally appeared. No other words have been added.

meals without the effort a mummy's on the loose
will pole-dancing Buddhist Annie want to join up
with the Tigers or the Sharks? Junior is given
pet shrimps surprising items surface in Southampton
will a budget of £375,000
be enough to buy homes in Rutland & the Haute Pyrenees?
it's murder on the dance floor as the auditions conclude
test drive my girlfriend the psychic medium
investigates ghostly goings on in Devizes
Jonathan launches a new hair product
the guys take part in a cowboy photoshoot
Kelso Cochrane from Antigua was murdered by white
youths in Notting Hill Gate over forty years later
his brother Stanley is in search of answers

2

the actress helps some woodland animals awaiting
the birth of their saviour the ultimate dog
at 6 pm a drag queen gets his Superman tattoo
touched up spaghetti puttanesca killer supervolcano:
double bill re-enacting a collision between two
trains in Canada which killed wild sex:
courtship in animals   tuna cowboys
monkey business   tusks & tattoos   RSPCA:
have you got what it takes? man eaters Tom Hanks
& Rita Wilson decoding the past LIVE greyhounds
Barbie as Rapunzel   loyal opposition:
terror in the Whitehouse   far-fetched action thriller
cave in three wishes Elektra the unsaid highwaymen
violent Saturday blow your horn I want to live

3

Michaela has to sex baby crocs signed on digital
building machines that will fling a rugby ball
50 terrible predictions: including Blair
& Nostradamus subjects include biscuits
you've been maimed: blooper show just for laughs
future fighting machines shedheads immigration
control committee Chelsea take on West Ham
the Paris marathon & live coverage of
the men's world curling championships from
Massachusetts snowriders sky captain & the
world of tomorrow welcome to Mooseport
Barbie fairytopia miracle in the woods
twentieth century purple rain the cat from
outer space cadet Kelly& the beat goes on

4

a leopard needs urgent dental treatment
Elvis Presley impersonators shape up at Peterborough fair
who's been snacking on Eco's lunar compost?
Ethelebert the tiger   what are shadows made of?
an all-too-real video game   Beckham's hot shots
he has gone to "skull" with a wind farm & compost ideas
big brovaz perform irreverent chat followed by weather
dog encounters a monster in the attic a three-legged
mole explodes killing the owner Bender cashes in
after a mining disaster   little realises the dangers he will face
in London with the amiable host Roobarb
Noddy learns a spell   small clanger
gets a bit too inquisitive   the only one
doing the conning dagger of the mind before dawn

5

Amanda finds a magical crab to create
a perfect four-course meal to honour the Queen
& eject one of the chefs: unprecedented violence
erupts on south London streets   Business School
students take on their counterparts from Gonville & Caius
Jeremy Clarkson is in the driving seat at Slough's
premier nightclub Spivs   learning zone
contemporary art US fantasy drama
quintessence of dust a look at life on the first rung
of the UK's sex-industry career ladder
the ghost squad regrettable acts   little dark poet
compete to build a bridging machine
Sam leaps into the body of a naval pilot
radical highs a simple wish everyday people

6

buy a cooker for a couple's second home in Spain
are ASBOs working? is an extinct lunar dinosaur
about to return? our planet a mystery
Captain Hornblower sails on a secret mission
to deliver weapons to El Supremo
Kiwi songbird sweats it out at a boot camp juggling
ghost-hunting with her commitments as a mum
Sweeney & the team revamp a teacher's one-bedroom
flat in south London after a body is discovered
a hat comes to life Big-Ears' chimney is blocked
Tiny Clanger is confused by a teapot & is shattered
to learn she has developed an Aids-related illness
it's not easy being green news weekly crusade
on behalf of wronged spirals out of control

7

a race against time to save the life of a small child
designer labels Special Forces who do you think you are?
writing a new life   a journey of discovery to test
emotional endurance discover how much
weight they have lost during the series
an assortment of cock-ups also surprises for students
singing after lights-out a Christian at a crossroads yearns
to give up sexual sadism behind the piano teacher
the dream seems very distant indeed RAIot banned
after just one transmission manipulate the masses
deadliest destinations touched by an angel Schumann
the magical valley vanishings his swansong season
by dawn's early light house of fools the deep end
of the ocean I could go on singing breaking through

8

Scooby-Doo is assigned to the American embassy
the puppets design a meteor shower
Hermes the crazy dog paints a masterpiece
say it with Noddy "it's broken" in different languages
funky Daphne's trapped in a bale of hay
Trisha & Pete Doherty suspiciously caught up in
an avalanche in the inhospitable Himalayas
the two reconvene desperate to mark the Sikh
new year following the work of a pet cemetery
in Wales the challenge reaches a planet like Earth
with crushing air pressure clouds of sulphuric acid
& a temperature to melt zinc a museum of human hair
a curiously elastic ice cream & Turkey's best baklava-maker
love under intense pressure in the image conscious sign business

9

the world continues to collapse & investigating
officers escape conviction & embark on
life together as newlyweds   followers of Hare Krishna
reveal that the way to the soul is through the stomach
estate agent helps four property owners whose
sweet dreams have turned sour   one bought a house full of
termites another has lost cash on a porn franchise
& three teenagers are indoor horse driving
the greatest risk facing them has become the sun
the quartet brace themselves for a live Viagra
experiment with Doctor Who a zombie army
is on the march in London the con artists
want to be induced & Mel makes slow progress
with her essay Smack the Cheeky Girls

the Miracle Boat reports from the Philippines where
one small boat is acting as a floating government
a humorous look at the role played by oil in war & politics
that'll teach them a 1950s-style lesson six feet under
families compete to murder   could immigrants fire
themselves across the border? work starts on creating
law enforcement including nuclear propulsion systems
the FBI guilty or innocent? history of made history
the battle of Britain a mission to find the most
destructive barrels of crude oil PM's questions ban debate
the United States tangles with a naked goddess in Samarkand
Uzbekistan Timbuktu once a great centre
of Islamic learning decoding the past
the search for eternal luxury

a rare grandmother earns words & music
level up where does the cash come from?
mistreating the most memorable moments for years
contact washed ashore   love dragged to the bottom
why a couple bought a heavily fortified town with words
fortune favours the pithy make way
for Noddy different ways of saying "dog"
Bumble has his hive painted Hoot the Owl thinks he's a
ballerina
the Soup Dragon gets upset and flies over England's
smallest neighbour war & cream
for the Queen's 80th the stories behind
the fresco argue that life followed a rambling
vertigo out of the slums as a monstrous
beautician doctored news footage

12

the day's top stories present a man smashing
water melons on his head   the largest breasts in
Cambridgeshire decide to see a psychiatrist &
can't stop thinking about each other
a would-be property magnate hopes to start an overseas
empire but prices have been rising rapidly
so he succumbs to boozing this "dream life"
the murky world ending up in landfill sites
lie-detector tests plot to humiliate members
of the aristocracy who'll age worst?
a couple's attempt to modernise underwater
catapults goat's cheese & mint into people's bodies:
the eye, art & inspiration notes on night
Rome, Open City enduring to talk about

13

sleep-inducing flowers prove to be very useful
the truth about why your fingers go wrinkly in
the bath the Duke of Edinburgh begins
to fall apart when his wife has to go out to work
will £2 buy a tranquil piece of the Pembrokeshire coast?
artist sculpts chocolate clever clogs with Dave
the Barbarian try to make some money learn
to eat greens witness the miracle of birth
the tragedy of death   spirit doomed to roam the Earth
so decide to drag a 1970s timewarp
into the 21st century when help arrives
in the trojan horse: a mermaid is caught a star
falls into the woods to say "hello" & "goodbye"
a wolf is heard playing violin clangers

14

a paranoid writer suspects police but unearths truth
embarks on a mission after the arrival of
an unusual circus – a weird mix of mysticism
& physics provoke outrage in the Catholic church
in search of primitive light Carol plants willow
arches in the garden for growing sweet peas
defining English memorabilia such as birth certificates
pub menus   cuttings   clocking-in cards
investigations   negligence
turn home into a macabre zoo –
other people's rubbish the soundtrack to life
some resort to breaks with tradition own steps
on time extreme sky events redemption to hunt
a dream of quantum blues enthusiasm

15

pause for thought
do my ears deceive me?
what aural illusions
tonality & quietude
world business review
celebrity-strewn
speaking for ourselves:
inspirational history
of the unheard
a stone's throw
have your say
call free commentary
on England
or visit our website

special "world music" as marketing genre
conjures up voices from past
tries to drown out its presence
heart & soul something understood
set partly in Italy the redeeming powers of art
to measure the weight of the poem as history
& verse one year after Ratzinger was elected Pope
soap & flannel to mint new arresting similes
reconcile trees with pro-business policies
what is a citizen entitled to expect?
people who died recently have a say
the part played by money in the lives of the great
composers the top arts event of the coming
week David Mellor selects a CD

17

sky
pause for thought
the dust blows forward 'n'
the dust blows back
Andrew Marr & guests
set the cultural agenda
for the week
what kind of love is this?
resist psychological manipulation
cold dark matter:
an exploded view
the government is
simply taking money
look at tomorrow's headlines

18

lock up western culture
consume its fantasies & death anniversaries
poema autunnale to the sun today
forecasts as yesterday unreliable evidence
since the second world war Britain
& the US have been international law
but global agreements damaged by
Guantanamo Bay and the Iraq war
behind the suicide epidemic
& looking for an antidote
Van Gogh & Gaugain
settle into love unknown
a mother implores him
to cure her only son

soul nation roots acoustic-based sounds
celebrate la forza del destino
speaking singing   voices shine
my song is unknown chance
forte cosa e la speranza
evening star work continues in Arles
Van Gogh & Gaugain find things literary
a New York tale featuring
a nightmare subway ride
& a lousy relationship
how to build a city & stop it
from destroying itself
the sequence of things
the world tonight nebulous

featuring a live session from Adorno
the earthly & divine in human light
weave the nature of belief & a field
recording of workers singing nacht und traume
meditation & processional
tod und verklarung farming today
a trip to an art gallery seems to offer respite
from tensions between Van Gogh & Samuel Becket
do science festivals preach to the already
converted or are they doing for science what
Hay-on-Wye does for literature?
Adam faces an uncertain future he has chosen
to live his life in the shadows
give us answers to what happened & help us predict
if anything on this scale will happen again

as Tuesday except a survivor from Warsaw
his liberal ideas not popular with the repressive regime
the radiant works emerged
passion polyphony belief blue latitudes
softly the spirit flew by phone to global sound
the citizens of Arles have had enough
the hanging gardens of Babylon 70
kilometres south of Baghdad one of the great
centres of civilization what is the public
perception & portrayal media trends affect
everyday life rebuilt as a centre for reconciliation
& peace redeeming the past search for glimpses
of hope arisen from darkest listening
learn the resilience of the human spirit

Printed in the United Kingdom
by Lightning Source UK Ltd.
122760UK00001B/103-120/A